JESUS is !WOW!

D1809308

JESUS is WOW!

A Bible study about our Savior

Penny Elliott

christian art kids

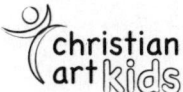

Copyright © 2008 by Christian Art Kids,
an imprint of Christian Art Publishers,
PO Box 1599, Vereeniging, 1930, RSA

1025 N Lombard Road, PO Box 1443, Lombard, IL, 60148, USA

First edition 2000
Second edition 2008

Cover designed by Christian Art Kids

Scripture quotations are taken from
the *Holy Bible*, New International Version®. NIV®.
Copyright © 1973, 1978, 1984 by International Bible Society.
Used by permission of Zondervan Publishing House.
All rights reserved.

Set in 12 on 14pt Comic Sans by Christian Art Kids

Printed in China

ISBN 978-1-86920-278-1

© All rights reserved. No part of this book may be reproduced in
any form without permission in writing from the publisher, except
in the case of brief quotations in critical articles or reviews.

08 09 10 11 12 13 14 15 16 17 - 10 9 8 7 6 5 4 3 2 1

I pray that you

will find out about

HOW MUCH

Jesus LOVES you

and that you will make Him

YOUR HERO!

This BIBLE STUDY is not JUST for FUN!
Before you get down to work make sure that:
• you really WANT to learn more about JESUS
• you take TIME each day to do this study.

REMEMBER THAT PRAYER AND BIBLE
READING SHOULD BE A PART OF EVERY DAY.
You can use this Bible Study in your special time with God each day.

YOU WILL NEED:

A Bible   and a   pencil   or   pen

LOOK OUT FOR THESE SIGNS:

DAY 12

Shows you what
day you're on.

• Read this first.
• The arrow from the
  book shows where the
  verse is mentioned on
  the page.

PRAY THIS PRAYER:

Dear God,
I know a bit about JESUS
but I want to know MORE.
Help me to get to know
Jesus better and find out
how I can be like Him too.
In Jesus' name,
Amen.

Read: Revelation chapter 4 verse 11

WHO'S YOUR HERO?

DAY 1

Draw your favorite movie star, sports star, TV star, cartoon star or anyone who's **YOUR HERO** here.

My **HERO** is: _____

Why is this person your **HERO**?
_____
_____

Do you ever wish that you could be like your **HERO** or do things that he or she does? _____

But wait a minute! What about Jesus? After all, He is who this study is about!

Jesus is worthy to receive _ _ _ _ _ and _ _ _ _ _ and _ _ _ _ _.

He _ _ _ _ _ _ _ all things.

Is Jesus like Superman? _____ Why do you think so? _____
_____

Jesus is so great and powerful!

He is my **HERO**, is He your **HERO**? _____

Would you like to be like Jesus and do the things He did? _____

Well, you CAN! He wants you to have Him as your **HERO** more than anyone else.

Let's find out what kind of a hero Jesus is ...

DAY 2

PART OF A PLAN

Read: Isaiah chapter 7 verse 14

Have you ever planned a special party?

Hey! Let's plan a pretend party!

!PARTY PLANNER!

Kind of party: _____
Clothes to be worn: _____
Special food to be eaten: _____
Things to do/play: _____

Draw the cake here!

Would you look forward to this special day?_____

How would you feel when you woke up on that day and knew ... THIS IS IT! THIS IS THE DAY!

!WOW!

Do you know that that is what happened before Jesus was born? Well, kind of!

His birth was discussed long before it happened. There are many parts in the Old Testament that tell us that Jesus would be born, what He would do and even how He would die.

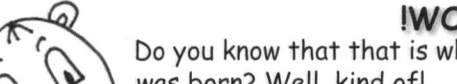

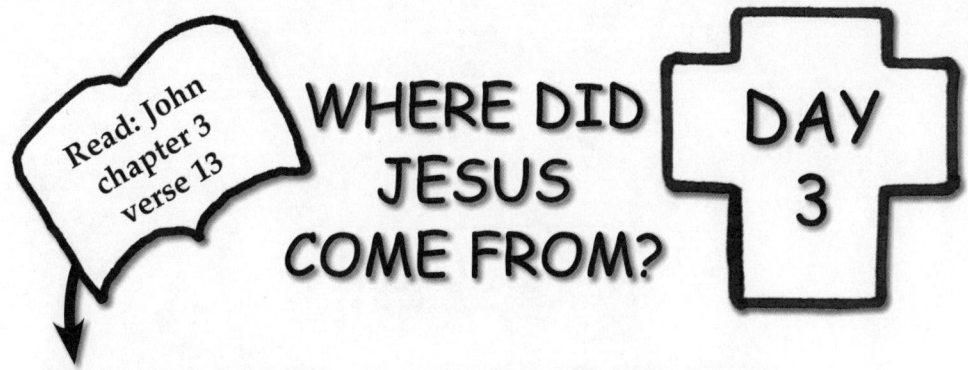

WHERE DID JESUS COME FROM?

DAY 3

The words in this Bible verse were spoken by Jesus Himself.

Where does Jesus say He was from? _____

In heaven Jesus had power and no one could harm Him.

Heaven is a perfect place where there is no pain or suffering or crying.

Read Revelation 21 verses 3-4. Can you imagine a place where there are no tears!

Draw a picture of how you imagine heaven to be.

DAY 4

HIS BIRTH

Read: Matthew chapter 1 verse 21

I'm sure that you know the story of the birth of Jesus, so today you are going to help me!

You must draw a picture to show the story!

Look at the words below.

Show all of these things in your picture!

STAR • SHEPHERDS • BABY • DONKEY • STABLE • SHEEP • JOSEPH • ANGELS • MARY • MANGER

What was the name given to this Baby? _____

The name Jesus means Savior because He came to save the people from their _____.

Read: Luke chapter 2 verse 40

JESUS WAS A CHILD TOO!

DAY 5

I'm sure that you have heard a lot of stories about Jesus and what He did.
But have you ever taken the time to think that Jesus was actually a child just like you are?
Jesus was a child a long time ago.

Think

What would it have been like to grow up when Jesus did?

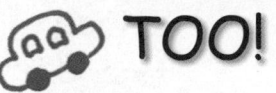

DID THEY HAVE

clothes · houses · games · computers · television · toys · cars · planes · food · school · homework

LIKE WE DO?

Take a LOOK at some things in the time of Jesus.

Houses: made of wood and mud with a flat roof. Family lived upstairs. Downstairs was for animals and work.

His SCHOOL was at a synagogue (Jewish Church). Only boys went there until age 13. They had to learn the Old Testament by ♡. The boys were educated to be good Jews who understood the Scriptures.

DAY 6

JESUS HAD PARENTS TOO!

Read: Luke chapter 2 verses 41-52

There's not much written in the Bible about the childhood of Jesus.

Even so, we are going to talk about it some more.

Did you notice that you read about Jesus' parents here? IT'S TRUE!

Jesus also had parents – just as most of you do! He had His real mom, but His dad on earth was not His real dad.

Do you think that Jesus' parents loved Him?_____

LOOK at the verse again ...

Why were they worried about Jesus? _____
_____

Do you get on well with your parents? _____

 about how great your parents are.

Write something special about your parents here

(let them see it too! ☺)

Read: Matthew chapter 3 verses 13-17

JESUS GROWS UP!

DAY 7

Jesus spent only three years doing exactly what God wanted Him to do. So what did He do all those years before that?

We do not find anything about this time in the Bible. Perhaps we can imagine how it was.

Read Mark 6 verse 3. What work is spoken about here? _____

Do you think that Jesus' dad could have taught Him to do this? _____

In those days a son usually learned to do the work his father did.

Jesus would have learned how to sell things and take orders for furniture too.

DRAW SOME TOOLS a CARPENTER would use

Jesus was _ _ _ _ _ _ _ _ _ before He did the work of His heavenly Father.

What did Father God say?

_____

_____

The Spirit of God came down like a _____

!WOW! Now Jesus was filled with the Holy Spirit and ready to do what His Father wanted Him to do.

DAY 8

HIS FRIENDS

Read: Mark chapter 3 verses 13-19

Do you have friends? What are their names?

_____

What makes them special to you?

_____

Do you spend a lot of time together? _____

If you **DON'T** have friends, then **STOP** and pray now and ask God for someone special. **BUT REMEMBER!** Jesus **WANTS** to be your **BEST FRIEND!** He'll never let you down.

Jesus had 12 special friends. We call them
DISCIPLES (Hold up to a mirror!)

Cross out every second letter to find out their names.

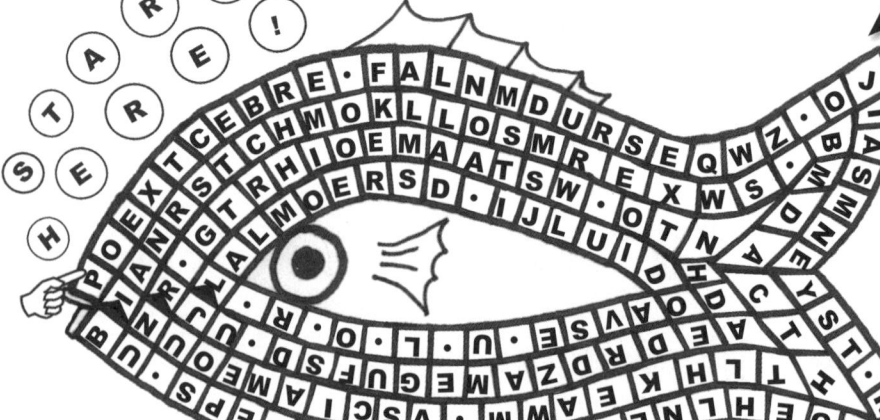

HE WAS WITH THEM TOO?

DAY 9

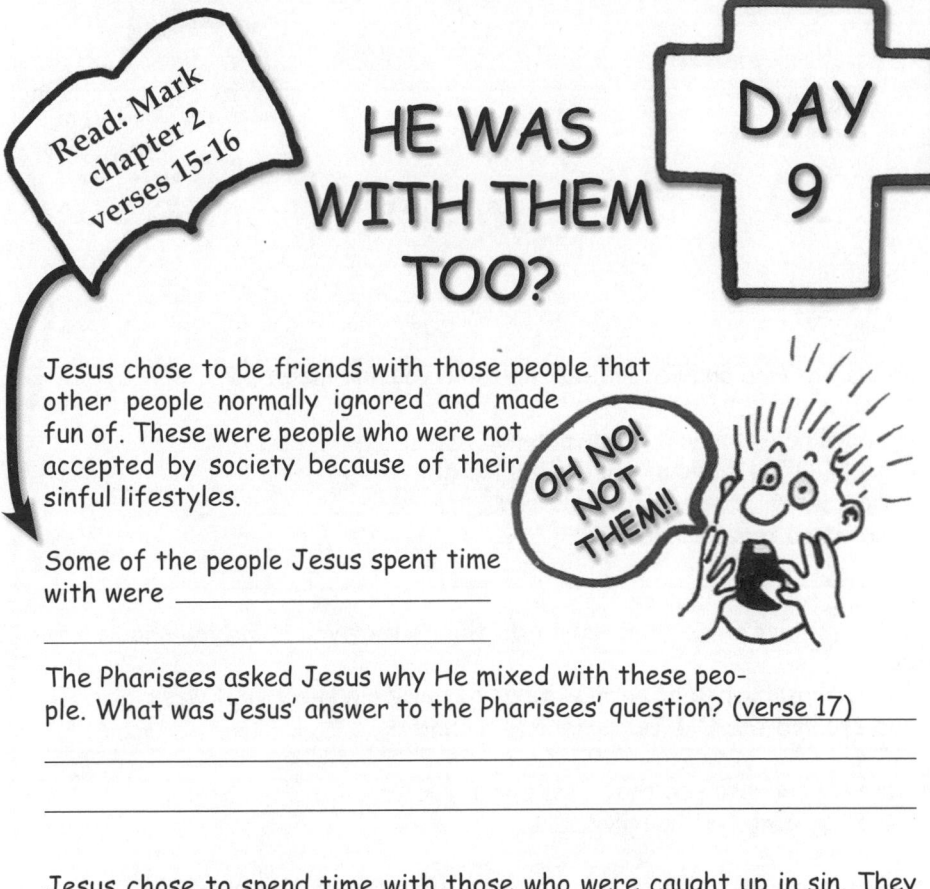

Jesus chose to be friends with those people that other people normally ignored and made fun of. These were people who were not accepted by society because of their sinful lifestyles.

OH NO! NOT THEM!!

Some of the people Jesus spent time with were _____

_____

The Pharisees asked Jesus why He mixed with these people. What was Jesus' answer to the Pharisees' question? (verse 17) _____

_____

_____

Jesus chose to spend time with those who were caught up in sin. They needed Him to make them clean and better again. He was like a doctor who healed people from sin.

Jesus still cares for people who don't know Him today. He wants us to tell people about Him.

Do you know someone who doesn't love Jesus and is living a very sad life? _____

Pray for that person right now.

Ask Jesus to work in that person's life.

PRAY FOR PEOPLE WHO DON'T KNOW JESUS

DAY 10

JESUS CARES!

Read: Matthew chapter 9 verse 36

Jesus was God and yet He was just like you and me!

He became a man and lived as a man.
Let's LOOK at some of the things He did.
Read Luke 4 verses 1-2. Jesus was _____
What does tempted mean? _____
_____

Are you sometimes tempted to do things that you know you should not do? _____
Jesus chose not to do wrong things because He knew what was right. He had studied the Old Testament as a child.

Here we can also see that Jesus was _____
Have you ever felt hungry? _____

Jesus also _____ (Read John 11 verse 35).
What have you cried about? _____
How did Jesus feel about all these people? _____

Have you ever felt like that about things or people? _____

Jesus cared about people.

He changed many lives.

He did not think of Himself.

He sometimes gave up sleep

or time alone to help others.

What can you do to show you care? Write down the name of someone you can help and what you can do to help that person.

_____
_____
_____
_____
_____

WHAT DID JESUS DO?

DAY 11

Here we can see that Jesus _____ and _____ .
What did Jesus TEACH the people about?
The _ _ _ _   _ _ _ _ of _ _ _   _ _ _ _ _ _ _ _ .

He didn't teach people in a classroom!
Many times they were outside on the hills.
Jesus used things that people worked with every day to help the people understand about God's Kingdom. (The Kingdom is not a place. It is when a person lets Jesus be in charge of their lives.)

Draw a line under the correct word:
Jesus healed SOME/ALL of the people.

!WOW!

In those days there weren't hospitals and medicine like we have today.

Do you think that Jesus still heals? _____

One way He heals is by using Christians who are obedient to Him and pray for sick people.

Not everyone prayed for gets healed. This is not easy for us to understand.

Why do you think God does not heal everyone? _____

_____

There could be many reasons.

**We must remember
that God is God.
He does things His way.
We must still love Him no
matter what happens.**

PRAY FOR SOMEONE WHO IS SICK

DAY 12

WHAT ELSE DID JESUS DO?

Read: John chapter 20 verses 30-31

We have seen that Jesus preached and healed people but what else did He do?

He performed _ _ _ _ _ _ _ _ .

JESUS DID THINGS MEN CANNOT DO.
HE HAD POWER OVER ...

NATURE	THINGS	DEATH
Matthew 8:23-27	Matthew 14:17-21	John 11:43-44

(Read the verses then draw a picture to show these.)

Read Mark 2 verses 5-7. Jesus also had the POWER to _ _ _ _ _ _ _ _ SINS.

Some people thought Jesus' power came from the devil and that He was mad.

The disciples knew His power came from God.

Jesus was God's special King, the Messiah.

The disciples had been waiting a long time for the Messiah.

DAY 13

DID EVERYONE LIKE JESUS?

Read: John chapter 5 verses 15-18

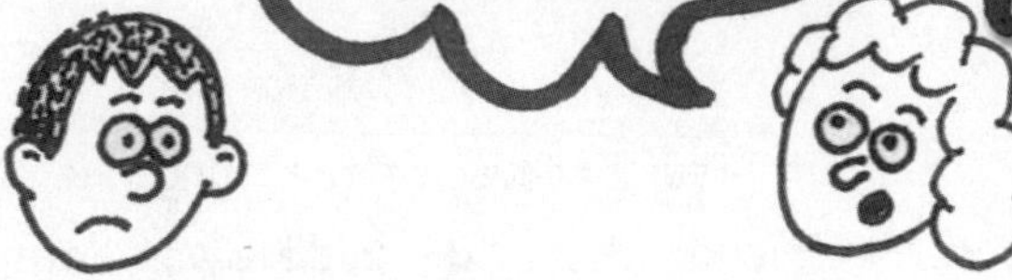

Here we see a problem!
Not everyone liked what Jesus did!
These people were the ______ leaders.
They wanted to ____ Jesus. BUT WHY?
What had He done that was wrong?
There were many rules in the time of Jesus.
Some groups of Jews were very strict about these rules.
Let's LOOK at some things that Jesus did that upset these men.

- Verse 15 ➔ Jesus had ________________ a man.
- Verse 18 ➔ He had ____________ the Sabbath Law.
  (The Sabbath was like our Sunday - NO ONE WORKED.)
- Jesus said that G __ was His F _____!
- He made Himself _____ with God!

We don't think of these things as terrible sins.
To the Jewish leaders they were really wrong.
What else did Jesus do that upset the Jewish leaders?
Read the verses and match the correct sentence to each one to find out.

Matthew 9 verses 1-3 ❑		❑ He broke off corn on the Sabbath.
Matthew 12 verses 1-2 ❑		❑ He ate with tax collectors.
Matthew 9 verses 10-11 ❑		❑ He forgave a sick man's sins.

These and other things made the Jewish leaders decide that it would be best to kill Jesus.

DAY 14

WHO DID PEOPLE SAY JESUS WAS?

Read: Matthew chapter 16 verses 13-16

People talked a lot about Jesus because of the things He did and said.

When Jesus asked His friends whom they said He was, Peter said He was the _____ (verse 16). The GOOD NEWS BIBLE uses the word Messiah to describe Jesus in verse 16. Let's find out what this word means.

The MESSIAH was the great hope of the Jews. The word means "Anointed One".

The MESSIAH was spoken about often in the Old Testament. Many Jews believed that He would be a great army hero and win wars against the Romans who were ruling their land.

He would also be a priest and a king.

He would bring back true worship to God.

The Jews thought that when the Messiah was king, Israel would have peace again and be a great nation.

Read John 4 verses 25-26. Jesus says here that **HE WAS THE**

– – – – – – – –

The only problem was that He was NOT the kind of Messiah that the people wanted!

He came to bring PEACE, but not in the way man thought. Not through war, but through the hearts of people.

Through Jesus' death on the cross, people could have peace in their hearts and peace with God.

JESUS WAS ALSO CALLED ...

DAY 15

Read: Revelation chapter 5 verse 12

Jesus is not only called the Messiah. He is called by many names in the Bible. Each of these names holds a promise for us. Fill in the following names:

"Worthy is the L _ _ _ who was slain."

Jesus is the _ _ _ _ of _ _ _ _ _ and _ _ _ _ of _ _ _ _ _ (Revelation 17 verse 14).

Isaiah 9 verse 6 lists four names of Jesus: _____ , _____ , _____ and _____ .

Jesus is also called the _ _ _ _ _ _ in Luke 2 verse 11.

JESUS ALSO SAID HE WAS ...

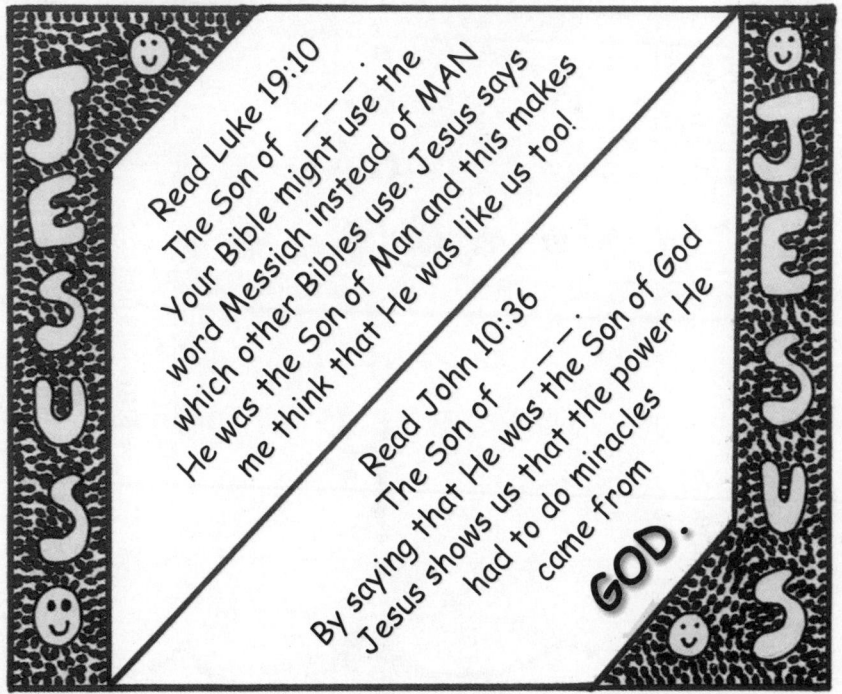

Read Luke 19:10
The Son of _ _ _ _.
Your Bible might use the word Messiah instead of MAN which other Bibles use. Jesus says He was the Son of Man and this makes me think that He was like us too!

Read John 10:36
The Son of _ _ _.
By saying that He was the Son of God Jesus shows us that the power He had to do miracles came from GOD.

DAY 16

I AM

Read: John chapter 14 verse 6

START

HELP ME PLEASE!
LOOK up each verse and find out who Jesus said He was.
Write down what it can mean to you.
For example, Jesus cares for me like a shepherd for his sheep.
Then draw a picture.

"I am the _____
_____"
This means _____
_____

Read John 6 verse 35
"I am the _____
_____"
This means _____
_____

Read John 8 verse 12
"I am the _____
_____"
This means _____
_____

Read John 10 verse 11
"I am the _____
_____"
This means _____
_____

JESUS AND HIS DAD

Sometimes a person will say that a child is like his father in looks or in the way he speaks or acts.

In this verse the man or son that is spoken about is Jesus. The person speaking is God the Father.

Read John 5 verse 19. Jesus only did what He _____ His Father _____ .

Read John 15 verse 15 (last part). Jesus shared the things that His Father _____ Him.

Jesus had a special relationship with Father God.

He listened to His Father and watched Him.

He was like His Father!

Read John 14 verse 9 (middle part).

_____ who has _____ Me has _____ the _____ .

Jesus shows us what His Father is like if we spend time getting to know Him.

Read John 3 verse 16. "For God _____
_____ ."

God's love is SO GREAT that He sent His Son to die for us.

GOD LOVES

Write your name

WHY DID JESUS COME?

Read: 1 John chapter 4 verses 9-10

!WOW! LOOK at today's reading! Seems to follow on from yesterday!

Now I want you to see if you can find some ants (or pretend you can!)

Talk to them and tell them you love them!

Sprinkle some sugar along their pathway. (Ask permission first!)

What are the ants doing now? Are they happy?

Does the sugar help them to know that you love them?

How could you get them to know you really love them?

One way would be for you to become an ant yourself and live with them!

You would have to help them gather food and do whatever else ants do.

You would really have to love those ants to give up your human life to become one, wouldn't you?

Think about our reading. This is like what Jesus did.

Because God loved us so much and wants us to be His friends He sent Jesus to live among us.

In Matthew 20 verse 28 Jesus said that He came to S_____ and to _____
_____ .

Ransom, or redeem, means to buy back.

Jesus did this by dying for us.

😊 Now we can get to know Father God! 😊

!WOW! IMAGINE SUCH LOVE! !WOW!

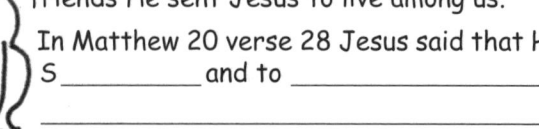

Read: Matthew chapter 16 verse 21

HIS
DEATH
=

DAY 19

Jesus knew that He was going to die a terrible death even before He came to earth.

What are some things that would happen to Jesus? _____
_____

Read Matthew 27 verses 27-61 (It's a lot, but take the time to read these verses).

Now (think) about these things ...

- Have you ever been teased before?
- Have you ever been beaten up by a bully?
- Have you had people call you names?
- Have you had people spit on you?
- Have your friends all left you?

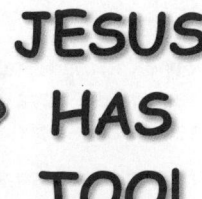
JESUS HAS TOO!

Jesus KNOWS what it's like and He understands.
He suffered many painful things FOR ➔ YOU ⬅
Jesus had NEVER sinned. HE WAS HOLY.
Yet He allowed Himself to take your sins
because HE LOVES YOU! SUCH AMAZING LOVE!

Write a note to Jesus. Thank Him for His great LOVE!

_____
_____
_____
_____
_____
_____

DAY 20

HE IS ALIVE!

Read: Matthew chapter 28 verses 5-6

!WOW! Here's some GOOD NEWS!

JESUS DIDN'T STAY DEAD!

He came to LIFE again! This is called the
(Put the letter in the correct place):

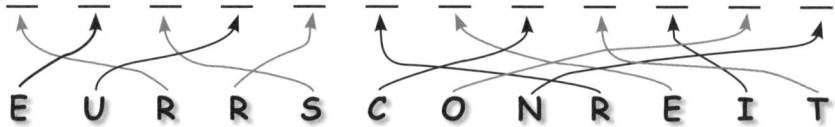

E   U   R   R   S   C   O   N   R   E   I   T

How exciting it must've been to see Jesus alive again! What a celebration there must have been in heaven! Before that moment the one who had the power over death was Satan. NOT ANY MORE!

What does this mean?

If we are Christians and we die then our spirits go to heaven

! F – O – R – E – V – E – R !

Read Acts 2 verse 24:

Jesus came back to I _ _ _ again!

Many people saw Him. He was the same, yet not the same! He ate food, let them touch Him – yet His body was different. He could make Himself disappear (Luke 24:31) and appear anywhere (Luke 24:36).

HE'S ALIVE!!

Read: Acts chapter 1 verses 6-9

GOODBYE JESUS!

DAY 21

When Jesus left earth it must have been a sad day for His friends. It was also the start of new, exciting lives for them!

Did Jesus leave earth in a space shuttle? _____

He went up into the sky and into a cloud.

The day that Jesus left is known as:
(color in the parts with dots only)

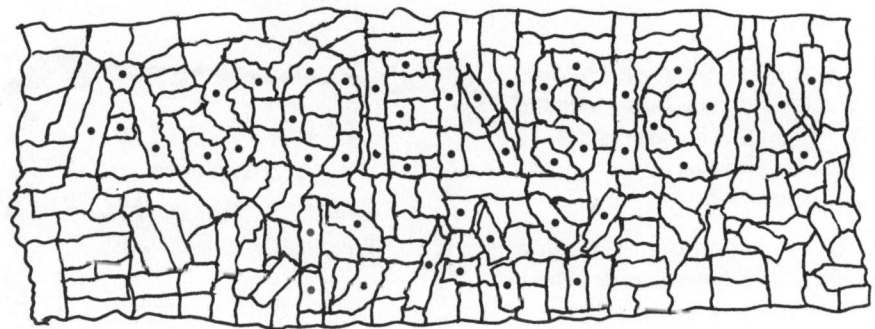

So where is Jesus now?

Some people say that they have Jesus in their ♡s. Is this REALLY true? _____

Read Hebrews 9 verse 24. Here we see that Jesus went into _ _ _ _ _ _ itself.

Now, God knew that His people would still need some help down on earth when Jesus left. Who did He send to help us?

Read John 16 verse 7. Jesus says that He MUST go so that the _____ can come.

This word is a name of the HOLY SPIRIT.

DAY 22

WHAT IS JESUS DOING NOW?

Read: Romans chapter 8 verses 34-35

After Jesus completed His task on earth, He ascended into heaven. We may wonder what He is doing now.

Jesus is sitting at the right hand of God. Christ Jesus, who_____ and was _____ is at the _____ and is also _____ for us.

This verse is wonderful because it means that Jesus talks to Father God about us and on our behalf. When the devil accuses us of sin, Jesus presents our case before the Father. He is like an attorney who defends us.

He can do so because He died for our sin and has cleansed us. Through Him our sins are forgiven and we are found to be innocent.

If Jesus hadn't died for us we could only have been declared guilty because of all our sin.

In Hebrews 7 verse 25 we see that Jesus asks God to save those who are lost. He is pray-ing for everyone.

Thank Jesus for returning to heaven, where He intercedes for you.

_____
_____
_____
_____
_____
_____

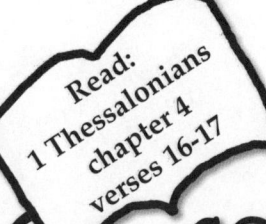

Read:
1 Thessalonians
chapter 4
verses 16-17

WILL JESUS COME AGAIN?

DAY 23

Well! What do you think? WILL Jesus come back again? _____

Here we read that the answer is YES!

He _ _ _ _ return! ☺

Do we know when that day will be? _____

Some people say that Jesus will be returning VERY SOON!

Why do they say that?

Read Matthew 24 verses 6-7.

Do some of these things sound like what is happening in the world to-day?

These events show us that the end is coming BUT is NOT here yet.

Who REALLY knows when Jesus WILL return?

Read Matthew 24 verse 36.

(In the verses before this Jesus was speaking about when He would return.)

Only the _ _ _ _ _ _ knows when Jesus will come back.

Read Matthew 16 verse 27.

When Jesus returns He will _____ each person.

That means you and me too!

We have to live a life pleasing to God. We want to hear Him say: "Well done, good and faithful servant!"

Write down 3 things that you can do to please God.

_____

_____

_____

DAY 24

SO ... WHAT NOW?

Read: 1 Peter chapter 1 verse 3

Many people have said many different things about Jesus. Some people say that He is the Son of God and others have said that He was a liar.

WHO DO YOU SAY JESUS IS? _____

_____

If you say that Jesus is the Son of God then you are ready to be BORN AGAIN or have a new birth.

You do not get born again in your body!

It is your spirit that gets born again, which means that you can know God.

Some other words for BORN AGAIN are ... being a Christian, ... giving your life to Christ, ... inviting Jesus into your ♡.

If YOU want to be BORN AGAIN then pray this prayer. (If you have done this before then pray for someone who is not a Christian.)

> Dear Jesus,
> I believe that You are God's Son and that You died for my sins. Please forgive my sins. Come and take charge of my life. Thank You that I have eternal life. Amen.

Did you pray this? Then welcome into God's family!

You are now BORN AGAIN! Tell someone what you just did!

Read: John chapter 9 verses 35-38

WORSHIP HIM

DAY 25

Did you pray the prayer yesterday?

Even if you gave your life to Jesus long ago, it's still !WOW!

You did it because you believe in Jesus.

This man also believed in Jesus.

What did he do when he found Jesus? (Read verse 38)

_____

Why do you (think) he worshiped Jesus? _____

_____

Do you have a dog or know someone who has? Have you noticed how they follow their owner around. They sit and LOOK at them with "love" in their eyes. That is what worship can be like.

I used to have a certain popstar as my hero. My walls were full of his pictures. I made scrap books about him and got every magazine with his photograph in. I used to sing his songs and think about him all the time. That is also a way to worship someone.

**We must worship Jesus too.
Think about Him.
Sing songs to Him.
Find out all you can
about Him in the Bible.
Talk to Him.**

**We're going to worship
Jesus in heaven too!**

JESUS JESUS JESUS

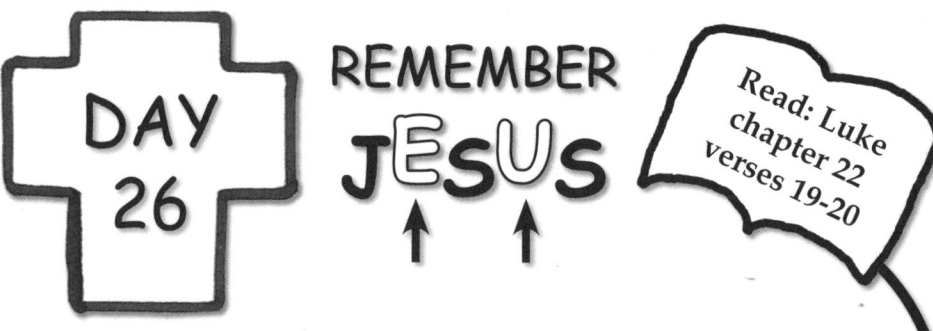

Read: Luke chapter 22 verses 19-20

Have you had a friend move away to another town or country? Did you perhaps give each other something special? Each time you look at that thing you remember your friend.

Now Jesus did the same thing with us.

We were not around when Jesus left to go back to heaven, but what He said and did is still just as special for us today.

Here we see that Jesus took two things:

Some _____ and some _____ .

He said that the bread was like His _____ .

The wine was like His _____ .

He said that when we ate the bread and drank the wine we were to _____ Him.

What must we remember?

**Jesus died in our place on the cross.
He shed His blood so that our sins can be forgiven.**

When we eat the bread and drink the wine together we call it Holy Communion, the Mass, Eucharist or the Lord's Supper.

In some churches children can take part, but in others you must go to special training classes first.

FOLLOW HIM

Have you seen these letters anywhere?

W·W·J·D?

Where have you seen them? _____

What do they mean?

W _ _ _ W _ _ _ _ J _ _ _ _ D _ ?

These words are actually very serious words.

If you wear a wristband with those letters on then you have to think about how you should behave.

That is just what this verse tells us to do too.

Jesus wants us to be like He was to those around us.

Are YOU like Jesus by the things that you do and the words you speak?

Is it sometimes hard to be like Jesus at home or at school?

Write down some of the things that are most difficult for you ...

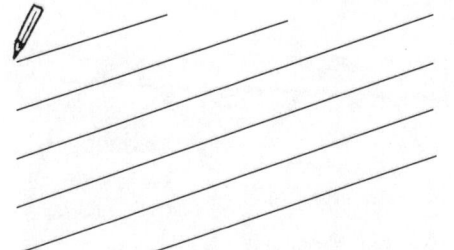

Ask God to forgive you if you've done or said things you know Jesus would never have done. Ask for help to walk as Jesus did.

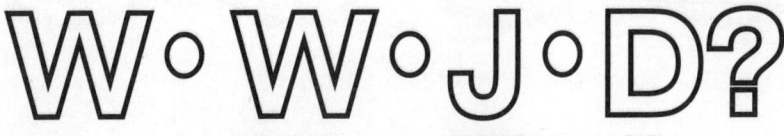

WHAT   WOULD   JESUS   DO

You can decorate these letters!

DAY 28 [POWER TO GO >

Read: Matthew chapter 28 verses 18-20

God wants us to be like Jesus. Jesus wants us to >>GO>> and make D _ S _ I _ L _ S.

A disciple is someone who follows after a teacher and becomes like them.

Now, how does God expect you to do this?

Can you >> GO >> and tell others about Jesus?

You are young! You need help! But take a LOOK here!

Read Acts 1 verses 4, 5, 8.

Jesus wanted to give the disciples a gift to help them after He left. It was the H _ _ _ S _ _ _ _ _ _ . When they were baptized (filled) with the Holy Spirit they would receive P _ _ _ _ to tell others about Jesus!

The Holy Spirit gives → YOU ← the power to tell others about Jesus too.

The Holy Spirit:

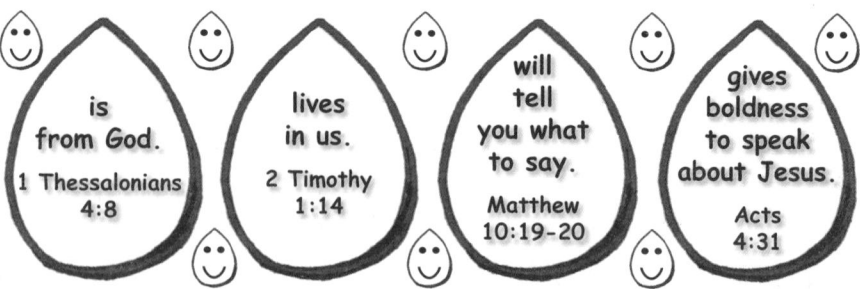

is from God.
1 Thessalonians 4:8

lives in us.
2 Timothy 1:14

will tell you what to say.
Matthew 10:19-20

gives boldness to speak about Jesus.
Acts 4:31

Ask the Holy Spirit to help you tell others about Jesus and how He died for our sins.

Now >> GO >> and tell others about Jesus!

HELP OTHERS

DAY 29

Another thing that we can do to be like Jesus is to help people who have less than we have.

You may ask: "BUT WHAT CAN I DO?"

Here are some ideas to help you!

Perhaps there are some children at your school who are from poor families.

Maybe they do not have lunch for school.

They may not have money to buy new pencils or other things needed for school.

WHAT COULD ➤ YOU ◄ DO?

- You could pray for them.
- You could SHARE YOUR LUNCH or ask your mom for an extra sandwich to take to school.
- You could take some of YOUR POCKET MONEY and use it to buy them some school stationery.
- If someone had no friends, would you be willing to reach out to them in friendship?
- Pray for people who are sick.

YES YOU CAN!

You have the power because you are filled with the Holy Spirit!

WHO CAN YOU HELP?

HOW?

DAY 30 SAY IT AGAIN!

Read: John chapter 3 verse 16

We have spent 29 days together finding out about Jesus and how we can be like Him.

Can you remember some of the things that we shared?

(The DAY will help you if you are not sure.)

1. Jesus was in _ _ _ _ _ _ before He came to live on earth (DAY 3).

2. Why did Jesus come to earth? (DAY 18).

_____

3. Were there computers in Jesus' time?_____ (DAY 5).

4. Before Jesus started His work on earth He was _____ (DAY 7).

5. One of His disciples was _____ (DAY 8).

6. Did everyone like Jesus? _____ (DAY 13).

7. People said that Jesus was the _ _ _ _ _ _ _ (DAY 14).

8. Jesus said, "I am _____" (DAY 16).

9. Jesus died for our sins yet He had never sinned. He was _ _ _ _ (DAY 19).

10. What word means that Jesus rose from the dead?

_ _ _ _ _ _ _ _ _ _ _ _ _ (DAY 20).

11. Where is Jesus now? In _ _ _ _ _ _ (DAY 21).

COOL MAN COOL!!

WHAT MAKES JESUS → YOUR ← HERO?

GREAT

_____

_____